BORDER AND IMMIGRATION CONTROL

Rescue and Prevention: Defending Our Nation

- Biological and Germ Warfare Protection
- Border and Immigration Control
- Counterterrorist Forces with the CIA
- The Department of Homeland Security
- The Drug Enforcement Administration
- Firefighters
- Hostage Rescue with the FBI
- The National Guard
- Police Crime Prevention
- Protecting the Nation with the U.S. Air Force
- Protecting the Nation with the U.S. Army
- Protecting the Nation with the U.S. Navy
- Rescue at Sea with the U.S. and Canadian Coast Guards
- The U.S. Transportation Security Administration
- Wilderness Rescue with the U.S. Search and Rescue Task Force

BORDER AND IMMIGRATION CONTROL

MICHAEL KERRIGAN

MASON CREST PUBLISHERS
www.masoncrest.com

Mason Crest Publishers Inc.
370 Reed Road
Broomall, PA 19008
(866) MCP-BOOK (toll free)
www.masoncrest.com

First printing

1 2 3 4 5 6 7 8 9 10

Library of Congress Cataloging-in-Publication Data on file
at the Library of Congress

ISBN 1-59084-408-4

Editorial and design by
Amber Books Ltd.
Bradley's Close
74–77 White Lion Street
London N1 9PF
www.amberbooks.co.uk

Project Editor: Michael Spilling
Design: Graham Curd
Picture Research: Natasha Jones

Printed and bound in Jordan

DEDICATION

This book is dedicated to those who perished in the terrorist attacks of
September 11, 2001, and to all the committed individuals who continually
serve to defend freedom and protect the American people.

CONTENTS

INTRODUCTION

September 11, 2001, saw terrorism cast its lethal shadow across the globe. The deaths inflicted at the Twin Towers, at the Pentagon, and in Pennsylvania were truly an attack on the world and civilization itself. However, even as the impact echoed around the world, the forces of decency were fighting back: Americans drew inspiration from a new breed of previously unsung, everyday heroes. Amid the smoking rubble, firefighters, police officers, search-and-rescue, and other "first responders" made history. The sacrifices made that day will never be forgotten.

Out of the horror and destruction, we have fought back on every front. When the terrorists struck, their target was not just the United States, but also the values that the American people share with others all over the world who cherish freedom. Country by country, region by region, state by state, we have strengthened our public-safety efforts to make it much more difficult for terrorists.

Others have come to the forefront: from the Coast Guard to the Border Patrol, a wide range of agencies work day and night for our protection. Before the terrorist attacks of September 11, 2001, launched them into the spotlight, the courage of these guardians went largely unrecognized, although in truth, the sense of service was always honor enough for them. We can never repay the debt we owe them, but by increasing our understanding of the work they do, the *Rescue and Prevention: Defending Our Nation* books will enable us to better appreciate our brave defenders.

Steven L. Labov—CISM, MSO, CERT 3
Chief of Department, United States Search and Rescue Task Force

Left: Today's Americans come from all parts of the world. Here, President George W. Bush, Jr. meets a group of newly naturalized citizens.

INTO THE MELTING POT

Across the world, the term "foreigner" often means someone to be feared and distrusted. In America, however, this is a foreign way of thinking. The notion of the "undesirable alien" is in a profound sense un-American: the United States has always been a nation of immigrants.

Often oppressed by poverty or political tyranny in their homelands across the oceans, our ancestors came here with the spirit to build a **democracy**. Indeed, people are the richest resource of America; diversity is a great source of its strength—as it says on the penny, E Pluribus Unum, "from many, one." In these dangerous times, however, such openness may also be a cause of vulnerability, an invitation to those who would exploit it for evil ends. Criminals, from small-time smugglers to large-scale narcotics traffickers and international terrorists, stand to gain the most by gaining illegal entry to the United States.

Those who stand to lose most are, ironically, the most recent immigrants, committed though they overwhelmingly are to their new homeland. Since September 11, 2001, and the attacks on New York and Washington, D.C., distrust of immigrants has—for the

Left: Built as a beacon of hope for the poor and oppressed of 19th-century Europe, the Statue of Liberty in New York has become perhaps the most instantly recognizable image of American democracy the whole world over.

As they gave thanks for their safe arrival at Plymouth Rock, Massachusetts, in 1620, the "Pilgrim Fathers" could little have imagined how many thousands of other ships would in time stream westward in the wake of the *Mayflower*.

most part unfairly, yet inevitably—grown. The great challenge of our time is to hold the line against our enemies, while welcoming our friends and fostering the international trade that is the economic lifeblood of our country. This most difficult of tasks falls on the men and women of the Immigration and Naturalization Service (INS) and the officers of the U.S. Border Patrol.

A HOME AWAY FROM HOME

The Wall of Honor at Ellis Island is a place of **pilgrimage** for many thousands of Americans each year. For generations, this little offshore complex in New York Harbor was the gateway to America. Thousands passed through each day as ships disembarked their passengers from distant ports worldwide. Between 1892 and 1947, an estimated 20 million immigrants successfully passed through to a new life and new opportunities. It is their descendants who come to the wall today, to remember and give thanks.

Immigrants have made America what it is today. The immigrant heritage is shared, in some shape or form, by the vast majority of

Eagerness, excitement, anticipation, apprehension, and hope: arrival in America meant a melting pot of emotions for foreign immigrants. Scenes such as this could once be seen just about every day beside New York Harbor, where no fewer than 10 million incomers disembarked between 1860 and 1890.

U.S. citizens, whatever their ethnic background. Even Native Americans originated elsewhere. In the course of the last Ice Age, they left Eurasia, crossing the "Beringia" land bridge (now the Bering Strait) to reach what is now Alaska. That was many millennia ago, of course; most of us can boast no such ancient roots in the land, being comparative newcomers, whatever our race or ethnicity.

The history of the United States is one of successive waves of **immigration**, as populations from different regions of the world

COMINGS AND GOINGS

In the year 2000 alone, no fewer than 489 million people passed through U.S. immigration controls, flying in on 829,000 planes or riding in 11.5 million trucks or 129 million passenger vehicles. This bustling activity on our borders, round our coasts, and at our airports has helped spell prosperity for America down the years. Freedom of movement and ease of transportation have been key to the country's economic success. In the context of September 11, 2001, however, such statistics can seem frightening. Any one of these individuals entering our country could have evil intentions. Yet how are we to find the terrorist needle in a haystack so vast and complex? If we close our borders, we play the terrorists' game— and impoverish ourselves and our overseas trading partners in the process. The challenge facing those entrusted with the task of maintaining our border and immigration controls is to develop "smart borders" that, while firmly closed to criminals and terrorists, will at the same time remain freely open for honest business.

Once these empty halls were thronged with anxious, expectant immigrants; once these echoing spaces rang with the babel of voices speaking in every language. Today, by contrast, they have the hushed air of a cathedral. The Ellis Island complex has become a shrine to America's multiethnic traditions.

came flocking to these shores. Historians make a distinction between two different types of immigrants: those "pushed" by problems at home and those "pulled" by the attractions of the host country. The Pilgrims of the 17th century were classically "pushed"—religious **persecution** in their English homeland sending them in search of a sanctuary across the Atlantic Ocean.

Other English colonists were "pulled," drawn by the prospect of rich and spacious lands for farming. African-Americans do not fit into either of these categories, of course. They were effectively

A WORLDWIDE WELCOME

Generations of American schoolchildren learned by heart the lines
by Emma Lazarus inscribed on the base of the Statue of Liberty—
thankful for the spirit of welcome that first inspired them:

> Give me your tired, your poor,
>
> Your huddled masses yearning to breathe free,
>
> The wretched refuse of your teeming shore,
>
> Send these, the homeless, tempest-tossed to me,
>
> I lift my lamp beside the golden door!

**New arrivals from Europe crowd round a table in the lunchroom
at Ellis Island in 1923. Would their next meal be taken in
America as documented immigrants?**

Polish farmer Josef Bujac, 28, his wife Zofia, and their daughter Krystina, arrived in Boston under the Displaced Persons Act of 1948. The end of World War II saw many millions of Europeans uprooted from their homes, their occupations gone, their families destroyed.

FROM PREJUDICE TO POGROM

The view that Jews were "Christ-killers" licensed their persecution throughout much of European history. They were herded into ghettoes and were then distrusted as a race apart. In reality, their only crime was to have fallen foul of people's perennial fear and suspicion of what they do not understand—and this made Jews an easy scapegoat when things went wrong.

In the empire of the Russian czars, **anti-Semitism** was a part of everyday life for centuries; and in times of economic difficulty, it flared up into full-blown pogroms. These were terrifying attacks against Jewish neighborhoods. Mobs vented their frustrations on what they saw as their ancestral enemy, burning homes and businesses and—all too often—killing people.

In the last decades of the 19th century, Russia's economic plight grew more strained by the year—and in the early 20th century, the country collapsed under the strain of famine, social upheaval, war, and revolution. This, combined with the continued violent persecution of the Jews, sent many thousands to seek refuge across the waves.

abducted from their homes and brought here unwillingly as slaves. By the end of the 19th century, increasing numbers of immigrants were flooding in from Eastern Europe, where Jews in particular were finding life intolerable.

America may have offered a lifeline to all these immigrant groups, but the benefits have by no means been only on one side. The

She may be officially only half-American (her father is a Mexican "alien"), but three-year-old Arely de los Reyes shows she is in no doubt herself about where her loyalties lie.

newcomers brought with them the skills (as craftspeople, farmers, artists, inventors, and so on) that they had acquired in their distant homelands. They also brought with them the immeasurable gift of energy. Their drive and enthusiasm gave enormous impetus to a fast-growing U.S. economy, an impetus which—thanks to successive waves of immigration—was ceaselessly renewed.

NO ROOM!

A New World it may have been, but America was not necessarily immune to all the evils of the Old. Even here, new immigrants encountered suspicion and prejudice. Like the countries of Europe, the United States had its economic cycles, its ups and downs—and immigrant workers welcomed in the good times might find themselves resented when recession came. Often, the worst offenders were those older immigrant groups that were yet to be finally established and whose own position seemed more precarious during economic downturns.

In the 19th century, a new understanding emerged. Although a country as vast as the United States might, in theory, have room for all, a modern, democratic society can develop only if all citizens are documented and all new arrivals registered in orderly fashion. The American welcome could hardly be expected to extend to hardened criminals or those suspected of being agents of hostile foreign governments, while dangerous diseases had to be excluded for the good of all. The floodgates, if not closed, were clearly going to have

Left: Xue Donghua pledged his allegiance to the American flag as part of his naturalization ceremony in March 2001, one of many thousands saved down the decades from political tyranny abroad. The importance of gaining "political asylum" is underlined by the case of Xue's wife, the distinguished scholar Gao Zhan, who has been detained by the Chinese authorities.

to be more carefully supervised. Serious immigration control was accordingly undertaken from the last decade of the 19th century.

BREATHING FREE?

Life was not necessarily comfortable for the country's immigrants. The possibilities of American life may have been limitless in the longer term, but most new immigrants found their immediate prospects severely restricted as they struggled to survive in the poorest quarters of a few big cities. Even in boom-times when jobs were available, there was always an abundance of U.S.-born labor competing to claim them; and when the crash came, there were always Americans on the lookout for an alien **scapegoat** to blame for their troubles. It was becoming clear that some sort of control would have to be taken of immigration—for the protection not only of America, but of the immigrants themselves.

The first serious acknowledgement at an official level that the flow of incomers to the United States would have to be policed and carefully controlled came in the 1880s.

Despite the best of intentions, the new bureaucracy became an object of fear for incoming immigrants; its ways were not always either sensitive or compassionate by modern standards. However

Left: Just off the boat in 1905, this Italian family has good reason to look apprehensive—the American "promised land" could be distinctly chilly in its welcome. But with the support of compatriots in the U.S., and with a willingness to work hard, many millions did succeed in realizing the "American Dream."

fondly it is visited now by their descendants, the "clearing station" on Ellis Island was regarded with considerable dread by the immigrants themselves, for entrance to America was by no means assured. After an intrusively thorough interrogation and an often humiliating physical examination, many were turned back from the country's doorstep on account of officials' (sometimes groundless) suspicions that they were bearing infectious disease or had irregularities in their papers.

For those excluded—at times as many as 20 percent of all

Whatever their race or birthplace, this INS citizenship ceremony marks the moment that these people officially become U.S. citizens through naturalization.

A WEST COAST WELCOME

Angel Island, in San Francisco Bay, served a comparable purpose for immigrants on America's West Coast. Many thousands of Chinese and other Asian immigrants passed through the center here. "I was really scared," admitted Jin Hua in a letter to her schoolfriend at home, Xiao Hong, in 1881. "Until this point, I had never seen such a variety of faces and skin colors. What if I get lost? What if something is wrong with me? What if I do not pass their tests? What if I am sent back? The what-ifs kept going through my head. Finally, after six hours, it was my turn to be checked. The inspector looked at me like some sort of strange bug. He checked my luggage (I had only one small trunk) as if he expected to find weapons in it. The man looked almost angry when the only things that he could find were my clothes—he checked those too—some books, and a photograph of my family. He took all the books even though I tried to explain that they were required for college."

applicants—there remained only the heartbreaking prospect of a return to what might now be a hostile "home." The prevailing atmosphere in a center where as many as 8,500 might be processed in a single day was, accordingly, one of bewildering confusion mingled with hope and—above all—profound anxiety. "To me it was like the House of Babel," Russian-born Barbara Barondess would recall a lifetime later. "There were so many languages and so many people. And everybody huddled together. And it was so full of fear, it was pathetic."

WHAT ARE AMERICANS?

Though in most respects an enthusiast for all things American, college student Jin Hua could still write sadly to a friend back in China, "Sometimes I feel that I do not belong here." She could hardly be blamed for having mixed feelings, given U.S. officialdom's apparent ambivalence toward her fellow Chinese. "A law was passed recently," she notes in a letter sent to her friend Xiao Hong in 1882, "that no Chinese can enter or exit the United States for the next 10 years." These were indeed the terms of that year's Chinese Exclusion Act; legislation in this period seldom bothered to conceal racist assumptions that did not shame white America at this time. The passing of the Immigration Act of 1891 put the rules on a more formal footing, but did nothing to change their discriminatory character. The Immigration Act of 1917, the Quota Act of 1921, and the Johnson–Reed Act of 1924 were unabashedly aimed at the exclusion of any but white Northern and Western European immigrants.

Racism is still very much a problem in America, as it is in other modern societies—although now, at least, it is generally regarded as a social evil. In the late 19th and early 20th centuries, however, racism was considered to be a thoroughgoing, scientific theory. If immigration control now has a bad name among some sections of

Right: Grant Avenue, San Francisco, a corner of the East on America's West Coast and heart of one of the United States' most famous Chinatowns. These old immigrant quarters exemplify the astonishing cultural richness of American society.

With the expert assistance of her grandmother, an eight-year-old girl does her Chinese language homework. The supposedly divided loyalties of "hyphenated Americans" were once a source of suspicion among the wider population; now children are encouraged to appreciate and explore their widely varied backgrounds.

the population, this is in large part due to the earlier **prejudices** and abuses of that time. Supposedly rigorous IQ (Intelligence Quotient) testing branded some races "less intelligent" than others. No allowance was made for the effect of cultural and linguistic factors on the findings of ineptly constructed tests. Put simply, white Anglo-Saxon immigrants passed these tests more easily than did other groups—especially non-Europeans. Immigrants from

WHERE TWO WORLDS MEET

Once, they came "tempest-tossed" from the "teeming shores" of Europe; now they trek north from the villages of Chiapas and beyond. But the same age-old economic forces are still "pushing" immigrants in the direction of America, a constant headache for those entrusted with the task of keeping order along the borders. Victor Manjarrez of the Naco, Arizona, Border Patrol is himself a Mexican American, and realistic about the endless streams of would-be immigrants attempting to cross our southern frontier illegally. "I think," he told *Time*'s Terry McCarthy, "we in the Border Patrol are getting better at what we are doing. But with a Third World economy to the south and a First World economic power to the north, we will always have this problem."

Stopped by an officer of the Border Patrol, a Mexican man suspected of being an illegal alien attempts to give an account of his presence on American soil. If his status is not legitimate, he will be apprehended and sent back to Mexico.

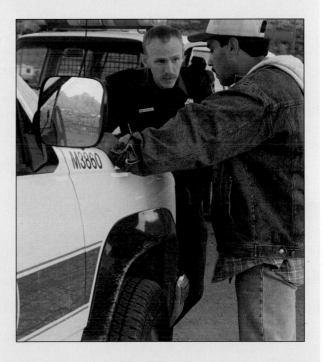

In a Deep South scene from the 1930s, African-American fieldworkers do for a pittance what their ancestors had been forced to do for nothing as bonded slaves. An exception among immigrant groups in that their passage was never voluntary, African-Americans have had to struggle harder than any other community for full acceptance.

Northern Europe found it easy to answer questions "correctly" when that "correctness" was very much dependent on a white Anglo-Saxon way of thinking. Other "researchers" ingeniously "proved" the superiority of the European to the Asiatic and African brain, arguing that white people were further evolved from their primeval "apehood." Such pseudo-science now stands completely discredited, of course; modern geneticists have left its findings in tatters. But the damage it did in its day was profound, and its consequences endure.

Racism has also led to other misjudgments. The **internment** of Japanese Americans at the time of the Second World War, for instance; not to mention the long and bloody struggle endured by African-Americans to claim their civil rights in U.S. society. Yet if America was initially slow to recognize its racism, it has striven hard in recent decades to make amends. Today's Americans are tolerant, as befits a nation of immigrants. Even now there may be tensions, however. Indeed, we see the old cycles still at work, with immigrants welcomed as cheap labor for farmers or affluent urban householders in the good times and resented as a drain on the resources of the nation when times are hard.

Despite these undoubted difficulties, all the indications are that immigrants will continue to settle in America—even if it may be a struggle to get established—while America will continue to thrive thanks to their contributions. If any refutation were needed of the grotesque absurdity of racist thinking, it is to be found in the extraordinary achievements of that unrivalled world superpower which might just as accurately be called the United Races of America.

THE MODERN MIGRANTS

America remains very much a nation of immigrants, with many thousands arriving every year, following in the footsteps of those who made their way in the course of the 19th and 20th centuries.

Stragglers from Britain and Ireland, Italy, the Scandinavian countries, and Eastern Europe still come to join well-established immigrant communities, and new waves of immigrants are flooding in from the Caribbean and Latin America. Many more have come across the Pacific from countries such as China, Vietnam, the Philippines, and India. The days of discriminatory policies for immigration are over. As before, some are "pulled" by the prospect of a better life; others are "pushed" by political upheavals in their home countries. America continues to offer sanctuary to many who might otherwise be in danger from dictators and their torturers elsewhere in the world. Today, although there may be tensions, Americans have a far better understanding of the contribution to be made by immigrants to the national life—their ability to make our nation not just more culturally colorful, but also more prosperous. Immigrants are, by definition, individuals of energy and enterprise: the whole nation gains from their hard work and creativity.

Left: Undocumented aliens line up outside the INS office in Chicago to regularize their positions under an April 2001 amnesty. Several thousand applications were received in response to a ruling that let naturalized citizens intercede on behalf of their relations.

Faces from around the world are to be seen at this INS naturalization ceremony in Atlanta, Georgia—a proud moment when another group of people makes the step from being an "alien" to full citizenship.

FACTS AND FIGURES

Each year, enough immigrants to populate a city settle legally in the United States. The figure for 2000 was 849,807. The number of illegal entrants can only be guessed at—current estimates put it at around 275,000 a year, with a total population of around 5 million undocumented immigrants. Five countries accounted for 39 percent of America's legal immigrants in 2000: Mexico (173,919), the People's Republic of China (45,652), the Philippines (42,474), India (42,046), and Vietnam (26,747). Mexico is believed to be the largest single source of illegal immigrants. An estimated

2.7 million undocumented Mexicans live here. A long way after this come El Salvador with 335,000, Guatemala with 165,000, and Canada with 120,000, by best current estimates. Haiti follows with 105,000 and the Philippines with 95,000. Other countries are represented too, from Ireland to India, and from Peru to Poland.

All these figures have to be set against those for **emigration**. Thousands of legal immigrants change their minds and decide to return to their home countries every year, while U.S.-born citizens leave to pursue lives and careers elsewhere. Despite this, however,

Cuban migrants wait on a bus prior to boarding a plane that will take them from Guantanamo Bay, Cuba, to Florida, in 1996. These Cubans are the last to leave the migrant processing center following a wave of migration to the base that started in August 1994.

the net trend is clearly upward. Large as these numbers are, they would make little impact if evenly dispersed through the United States. Immigration, however, tends to be concentrated around a number of major centers. Of legal immigrants into America in 2000, for instance, some 68 percent settled in six key states: California (217,753), New York (106,061), Florida (98,391), Texas (63,840), Illinois (40,013), and New Jersey (36,180).

THE NEW AMERICANS

Today's immigrants may come from very different parts of the world than their predecessors and from very different cultural backgrounds, but their response to the immigrant experience has been strikingly similar. They have tended to congregate in particular quarters to keep one another company in a strange society. For instance, New York's Chinatown and Little Italy have been joined by a distinctly Korean K-Town; while Miami's Little Havana is famous the world over.

The New Americans also share with their immigrant predecessors an indomitable work ethic and will to succeed, which makes light of challenges that would discourage more established, more comfortable communities. Immigrants have historically been willing to work long hours, forgoing luxuries and leisure time, in order to be able to hand on the benefits of a better life to their children. The spirit of self-help runs deep in immigrant communities. Far from "milking" welfare or health care services, the opposite appears to be the case. A study published in 2001 by the National Academy of Sciences quite clearly showed that the average immigrant pays

In a small Los Angeles store, a shopkeeper prepares traditional
Chinese herbal remedies, keeping alive a wisdom handed down over
generations. Every group that has come to America has brought with
it a cultural inheritance that benefits the whole of U.S. society.

MAKING GOOD

A Korean immigrant in New Jersey, Haesu Choi spends 2–3 hours each evening giving her two sons, ages 10 and 8, extra coaching with their schoolwork. "They complain that their friends get to watch TV," she told Heather MacDonald of the *New York City Journal.* "But I tell them because we're Asian, they have to do better." To the great benefit of America throughout its history, successive immigrant groups have all been driven by a desire to succeed—but even by these standards the Koreans are something special.

Though many have come to America with university educations, they have been prepared to work long hours for low wages in menial trades. Slowly, they have come to thrive. No fewer than 20 percent of America's dry-cleaning businesses are now Korean-owned. In southern California, 45 percent of the liquor stores and 46 percent of small supermarkets belong to Koreans; while in parts of Manhattan, they own 75 percent of the grocery stores. Koreans have been a presence in America for over a century, but in the past few decades their numbers have grown, with substantial Koreatowns springing up in several cities—most notably Los Angeles.

Left: A Korean-American girl snatches a quiet moment to herself as she eats noodles in a restaurant. Life starts getting serious early in America's Korean community: children have little time out from work and academic study.

His worldly possessions in two plastic bags, his child in the sling at his chest, a father in the former Yugoslavia sets off to face an uncertain future as a refugee. Many thousands of men, women, and children from the former Yugoslavia have found sanctuary in the U.S.

A LONG JOURNEY

Isaac Borenstein's life story provides a short course in 20th-century history. His family lived in Poland before the Second World War. Most of his relations were destined to be murdered in the Nazi Holocaust, but Borenstein's branch of the family fled to Havana, Cuba, where Isaac was born in 1950. When Fidel Castro's Communists took power, they were forced to flee again—this time to the United States, to Nashville, Tennessee.

What he found in the **segregationist** South both confused and shocked the young immigrant. As both a Jew and a Spanish-speaker, he felt rejected; and the "whites only" water fountains were, he felt, an ugly stain on a "wonderful country." Determined to serve both his adoptive country and the cause of justice, he went into the law, and since 1986 has served as a judge in Boston.

Borenstein sees America's imperfections clearly, but in the end there is nowhere else he would want to be. "I'm very corny about democracy," he admitted to Stan Grossfeld of the *Boston Globe Magazine.* This is his homeland, he says: "I'm incredibly proud and grateful."

$1,800 more in taxes than he or she receives in benefits each year.

However much the immigrants may gain from America, then, America gets more in return—even in the most down-to-earth economic terms. Once the calculation is extended to include such intangibles as the energy and ingenuity of the immigrants, the balance of benefits shifts overwhelmingly in America's favor.

SAFE AT LAST: ZO T. HMUNG

The brutal coup of 1962 put an end to democracy in the Asian state of Burma—for the Chin people it also brought religious persecution. A Christian minority in a predominantly Buddhist state, they were regarded with especial suspicion by a military government that had a ruthless way with those it saw as troublemakers. When the Burmese pro-democracy movement took off from 1988 onward, many Chin played an enthusiastic part. One such, Zo T. Hmung, campaigned underground in Burma for several years, but was eventually forced to flee across the border into India, where thousands of exiled Burmese were already living.

In 1994, however, the Burmese and Indian governments signed a cross-border cooperation agreement, under the terms of which many hundreds of Burmese refugees were to be rounded up and summarily returned to their homeland—and to the none-too-tender mercies of an angry government. Facing the prospect of returning home to a certain death, Zo T. Hmung fled again, this time to the United States, where he was granted political asylum.

Continuing his campaign for democracy in Burma, he was shocked to learn that back in India, his wife and children were on the brink of being returned home—where they would effectively be hostages of the Burmese government. Thanks to the intervention of a number of agencies, they were released by the Indian authorities. On September 1, 1998, the family was joyfully reunited at New York's John F. Kennedy Airport, to begin a new life in the United States.

Forced into flight by persecution in their native country, these children are Burmese Muslims who have taken refuge in the compound of the UNHCR in Kuala Lumpur, Malaysia.

INGENIOUS IMMIGRANTS

The economic contribution made by immigrants is clear, but what about the claim that they contribute creativity and enterprise to their adoptive country? Some years ago, to test the truth of this theory, the Alexis de Tocqueville Institution (AdTI) carried out a novel study, which worked out the proportion of U.S. patents taken out by immigrants to the country. A patent is the claim staked by inventors to any innovation they have created, and it registers that invention under the law. Analysis of the patents register thus lets researchers get a snapshot of cutting-edge technology at any given time. Taking 250 randomly selected recent patents, the AdTI went on to trace the background of the inventors, discovering that 48 out of 250—or 19 percent—were immigrants. As a proportion of the U.S. population, recent immigrants represent only 8.7 percent, so the implication is that they are contributing over twice their share.

A PLACE OF SAFETY

Of those granted U.S. citizenship in 2000, 65,941 were classed as **refugees** or asylees—people forced to flee their homelands by political developments there. With so many wars in the world and with so many tyrannical regimes, there are many men and women with what the Statute of the United Nations High Commissioner for Refugees (**UNHCR**) calls "a well-founded fear of persecution." Governments have, by international agreement, a legal duty to provide political **asylum** for those in this position—although asylum-seekers must first satisfy their prospective host that their "fear of persecution" is indeed "well-founded."

Hispanic immigrants wait at a parking lot in Silver Springs, Maryland, in the hope of being hired for a day's labor. Immigrants to America— especially illegals—know they will be expected to work long hours, doing the most tiring and dangerous jobs, for the lowest pay.

In the United States, the Immigration and Naturalization Service (INS) is responsible for ruling on applications in what has become an increasingly controversial area. Across the developed world, asylum applicants have been regarded with increasing suspicion by those who believe they may be motivated more by a desire for economic betterment than by genuine persecution. The fear that public goodwill may be cynically exploited by the undeserving has caused that goodwill virtually to disappear in several European countries, with vociferous campaigns against (and vicious racial attacks on) asylum seekers.

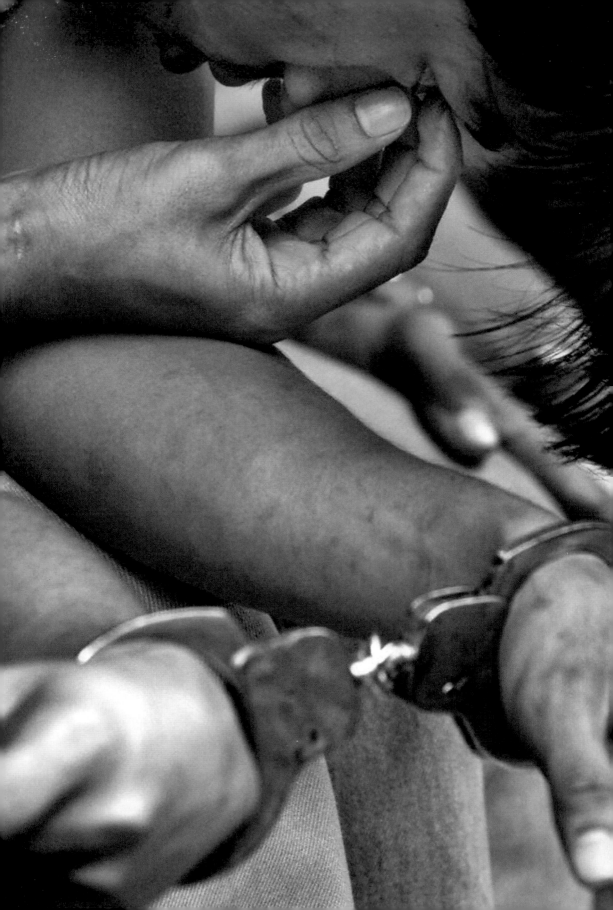

THE INS TODAY

The Immigration and Naturalization Service (INS), an agency of the United States Department of Justice, is the office charged with the task of administering America's immigration laws. Prior to its inauguration, immigration itself was policed by the Immigration Bureau, while a separate Naturalization Service supervised the programs by which new immigrants took the steps to full naturalization as U.S. citizens.

The merger of these two agencies in 1933 offered clear administrative efficiencies, but it also exemplified a new and more imaginative official philosophy on the immigration issue. The new agency could take a longer, more positive view; although rigorously upholding the law, its agents could consider potential immigrants as individual men and women and families. Conscious of the contribution immigrants might make to their adoptive country, the new service saw immigration less as a threat and more as an opportunity to be carefully managed for the good of all. No one stood to gain more from the proper supervision of procedures than the immigrants themselves, all-too-vulnerable in the past to exploitation. From smugglers and ship owners in their home countries to unscrupulous landlords and employers in the United States,

Left: An illegal immigrant from Indonesia is held in handcuffs to prevent his escape. Shocking as it may seem, such aliens have to be guarded as the criminals they are.

The Commissioner of the Immigration and Naturalization Service, James Ziglar, speaks to staff at the Arlington, Virginia, District Office: INS agents regard their work as an important moral mission.

there had never been any shortage of wrongdoers ready to take advantage of the victims of a poorly managed immigration system.

JUSTICE FOR ALL

The INS takes its status as an agency of the U.S. Department of Justice extremely seriously: to be just and fair in their treatment of America's immigrants is their ideal. As the office charged with the enforcement of the country's immigration laws, it has duties extending far beyond that of simply excluding illegal entrants. It has

FULL AND EQUAL PARTICIPANTS

The new emphasis in INS thinking cannot be more clearly indicated than by the recent recruitment of outgoing Acting Executive Associate Commissioner Barbara L. Strack to head up the National Immigration Forum's (NIF) recently established Center for the New American Community. The aim of the NIF is to see that America's tradition of openness is upheld and that the country continues to offer a welcome to immigrants of energy and enterprise. To this end, it sets out to provide not only guidance for new immigrant groups, but also support for those wider American communities that have to absorb them. "I am delighted with the opportunity to work with existing and emerging immigrant communities as they take their place at the table of American opportunity, and to ensure that cities and towns have the resources and the knowledge to make America as welcoming a place for newcomers as possible,"

said Strack on her appointment in January 2002. "There are both tremendous opportunities and important challenges for the newcomers and the communities that receive them."

Sharice Bradford and Mike McLaughlin sort numerous applications at the INS's Chicago office.

to administer all those processes by which legal immigrants are admitted and, eventually, naturalized as U.S. citizens. An INS agent might quite easily go through a lifetime's service without ever seeing a frontier. Much of the office's work is done in those urban and rural communities in which America's immigrants live and work. The organization of work permits and other papers, help with benefits and health care concerns—these are all part of the process by which "foreign" incomers become "New Americans."

STRUCTURE

The INS headquarters in Washington, D.C. oversees the work of three regional offices across the United States, to which a total of 29,000 staff working at 33 district offices all report. Moreover, another three district offices and 39 area offices outside U.S. territory give "Global Reach," meaning that much of the INS's work is carried out "at arm's length" in countries of origin around the world. From Johannesburg to Copenhagen, from Lima to New Delhi, there are agents in place to oversee applications for immigrant papers. The agency is thus in a position to be able to tackle many potential problems at the source, with incalculable benefits down the line for hard-pressed officials working on America's land frontiers and at its seaports and airports.

But bona-fide immigrants gain, too. Those whose claims to a place in U.S. society seem good can have their passage smoothed, while those deemed undeserving can be dissuaded from embarking on a futile (and sometimes dangerous) journey. A properly managed admission procedure necessarily involves a good deal of paper-

Members of a 57-strong party deported from America by the INS, these undocumented Guatemalans are interviewed by immigration agents on their arrival back in Guatemala City.

work—the more that can be taken care of beforehand, the better for the immigrant. The new arrival in America will have quite enough to think about without having to undergo a protracted—and inevitably, at times, frustrating—induction process.

COMMUNITY PROGRAMS

In recent years, the INS has increasingly been working with immigrant groups already established within the United States to

A sense of culture shock is expressed in the wondering eyes of these young boys, members of a Kosovo family just arrived at McGuire Air Force Base, New Jersey. All 450 refugees on board the flight from Macedonia were given temporary housing in the locality.

THE INS ON WHEELS

The INS in the San Diego sector of southern California has found a creative way to meet the people, thanks to its Mobile Community Storefront (MCS). A 30-foot (9-m) self-contained trailer converted into a traveling community-relations office, it enables agents to take the INS message to the most isolated reaches of the region. Visiting outlying districts in rotation, each time setting up for two weeks or more, the MCS has two highly qualified agents to offer guidance.

Many immigrants—especially Latinos—are employed on farms and ranches in remote rural areas, from which a visit to a big-city office would be a virtual impossibility. Now, the most far-flung communities have their chance to be at the center of things—for many, the MCS has already proved a valuable lifeline.

promote dialogue with government and the wider community and to improve services. Experience has shown that when immigrants themselves are helped to gain a fuller understanding of government policy, they feel empowered as full participants in American society.

On the other hand, since no one can hope to have a better sense of the immigrants' situation than the immigrants themselves, their input can be of incalculable value when it comes to developing policy. With their unique experience and insight, the INS may also have a constructive role to play in mediating between immigrant groups and their wider communities. Specially trained agents in many districts are available to give presentations and seminars in

Kurdish refugees from northern Iraq are received at Andersen Air Force Base in Guam, as part of the massive assistance effort, Operation Pacific Haven. Some 2,000 refugees were brought to the island in 1996 for processing, before being allocated housing in various places on the mainland of the United States.

schools, church halls, youth clubs, and other such places to explain INS policy on matters of current community concern.

At a more formal level, the INS holds regular meetings with the diplomatic representatives of countries of origin at their consulates in U.S. cities and with interested organizations, like the American Immigration Lawyers' Association. The more clearly official policy is understood, the easier it makes matters for all concerned.

A FOREIGN LANGUAGE

The greatest difficulty faced by most new immigrants is that of finding reliable information in a form in which they can clearly understand it, and INS "outreach" programs have a crucial role to play here. Nationally, the INS publishes literature not only in English, but also in Spanish, Chinese, Vietnamese, and Thai to help immigrants through what can be the intricate ins and outs of immigration law. Even when their applications have been officially approved, immigrants may find themselves unsure over the precise procedures of their naturalization programs.

Sensitive to such problems, staff at the INS's Chicago district office have made a concerted effort to reach the city's immigrants through their own community media, with contacts in over 50 different ethnic media organizations. Thus, INS agents contribute columns providing immigration information to a range of local newspapers catering to Spanish, Korean, Polish, Filipino, Chinese, and Romanian readers. Agents work with ethnic TV stations and appear regularly on Spanish, Polish, and Chinese radio phone-in shows to answer questions. Not content with such appearances, however, Chicago staff also have established their own cable TV show, *Ask INS,* which immigrants may call to have their questions answered live on-air.

EXCLUDING THE UNDESERVING

Important as all these activities are, the INS does have a responsibility to uphold the law. The prevention of illegal entry is, inevitably, an important aspect of its work. This involves not only border checks, but also inspections at docks and airports, as well as at workplaces suspected of employing illegal immigrants. On construction sites, farms, and in countless other situations, illegal immigrants may be exploited by unscrupulous employers aware that such workers are in no position to complain about poor pay or conditions. Undocumented workers all-too-often end up risking their health—even their lives—when compelled to work with toxic chemicals or inflammable materials, or when asked to perform otherwise hazardous tasks without adequate protection. Nobody but the corrupt employer benefits from working practices that jeopardize the safety not only of the immigrants themselves, but also of other workers and the general public.

The economic impact of illegal immigrants is easily exaggerated; they tend to do the dirty jobs that American workers are reluctant to do. But there is some truth in the claim that the presence of cheap illegal-immigrant labor may tend to drive general wage-levels down. The unjustified drawing of benefits by illegal immigrants is certainly an economic drain on the nation as a whole. In many such scams, the immigrants themselves are victims, exploited by ruthless criminal gangs that have the resources to forge false documentation.

With no official existence in the United States, the illegal immigrant is vulnerable. An important part of the INS's work involves the investigation and apprehension of organized "people smugglers." Cynical, sometimes murderous, exploiters of the desperate, such gangs offer to get people into America from China, Russia, or elsewhere—but always at a price. Those immigrants who do not die in an airless container, or who are not crushed by the

Detained by INS agents in El Centro, California, these undocumented Chinese immigrants have plenty of leisure to play cards, their plans to work in America's illegal labor market frustrated by the vigilance of the INS and U.S. Coast Guard.

JOURNEY OF DEATH

On June 19, 2000, customs officials at Dover, England, made a grisly discovery. They opened up the back of a truck, which its driver claimed was loaded with tomatoes. Behind a makeshift frame, which was loaded up with boxes of the fruit, they found a dreadful cache of human bodies—58 in all. Incredibly, there were also two survivors. Although traumatized, they were able to tell their tale.

The 60 Chinese refugees had been herded into the truck by criminals in a warehouse in Rotterdam, Holland. They had paid gangsters in their native China to smuggle them to Europe, where they hoped to build a better future for themselves and their families. For a time, their journey had gone according to plan; conditions in the back of the truck were appalling, but endurable. Then the tiny air vent, previously open, was sealed. The Dutch driver, Perry Wacker, afterward admitted to having closed it before driving on to the ferry at the Belgian port of Zeebrugge. The reason? He was concerned that alert officials might hear sounds to suggest that he was carrying a human cargo. With no source of fresh air, the refugees died an agonizing, terrifying death.

In recent years, Europe has been almost as sought-after a destination as America, many thousands of refugees entering through the Balkans, or across the Mediterranean through Spain or Italy. In early 2002, a Romanian gang caught in northern France was found to have been tampering with railway signals, stopping Eurostar trains and then concealing refugees on board for the journey through the Channel Tunnel to Britain.

In August 1999, 193 Asian migrants planning to enter the United States illegally were arrested by Canadian immigration agents in Gold River, British Columbia.

shifting cargo in a ship's hold, can find themselves virtual slaves on their arrival. Forced into degrading drudgery to service a debt, they are unlikely ever to glimpse the promised land.

By comparison, perhaps, the Mexican land-border holds fewer obvious perils—although an estimated 400 attempted immigrants die there every year. Some suffocate in the backs of trucks; others are hit by cars or fall from trains, while many are drowned when swept away by rain-swollen rivers. Here, too, there are predators ready to take advantage of these impoverished individuals. The aptly named **Coyotes**, human wolves of the border region, prey upon the pollos, or "chickens," as their defenseless clients are known.

TROY NEWMAN TO THE RESCUE

Racing through the Arizona Desert in an Agency 4 x 4, Agent Troy Newman brakes hard at the spot where a group of men has been found, quite clearly lost and exhausted. One has collapsed unconscious. In a temperature well over 100°F (38°C), this is no time to be walking across one of America's least hospitable regions. They are obviously illegal immigrants, but—as Troy explains to Tim Vanderpool of the *Christian Science Monitor*—there will be plenty of time for all those questions later. "Our goal here, first and foremost, is to respond to any emergencies," he says. Although ultimately an employee of the INS, Troy is first and foremost an Emergency Medical Technician, a member of a **BORSTAR**—a Border Patrol Search, Trauma, and Rescue Team. There are around 100 EMTs in all, with outposts spread out along the Mexican border. Even so, it can be hard to help a person who has gone to some trouble not to be seen. Although more than 2,000 men and women were rescued in 2000 by teams like Troy's, many are never discovered—and with those that are, it is a race against time. "We always hope we can get to them while they're still alive," says Troy. "That's what our job is about."

This sign on the U.S. border in southern Arizona reads: "Beware! Don't expose your life to the elements: it's not worth it!" Sadly, all too many Mexican and other migrants disagree. The warnings are well-founded: many die each year from exhaustion and exposure.

HOLDING THE LINE: THE BORDER PATROL

The protection of America's frontiers is essential if a just and consistent immigrant policy is to be maintained: no one stands to gain from a free-for-all. Large numbers of undocumented aliens create tensions between legitimate immigrant groups and their wider communities, and their presence is a potentially crippling burden on welfare and public-service budgets funded by all American taxpayers. Yet there are other reasons why the integrity of America's boundaries must be maintained: cross-border smuggling can cause untold damage, both to the economy and to society.

The consequences can be grave enough when smuggling is merely a matter of unpaid duties on manufactured imports—but often, of course, contraband goods are inherently dangerous items. The increase in the use of illegal narcotics has been one of the great social evils of our time, and our borders are a major frontline in the War Against Drugs. Along with these factors, another question must now be seriously considered: are America's borders, in effect, an open door for international terrorists? The attacks of September 11,

Left: The most formidable frontier defenses cannot keep out the truly determined illegal immigrant. If they are caught and deported, they will simply turn round and try again. The Border Patrol may have the expertise and equipment, but the aliens have the numbers—with thousands crossing over nightly, some will always get through.

2001, have brought home to us the likely costs of complacency. The United States must stand alert to exclude those elements that would do it harm. For all sorts of different reasons, then, the work of the Border Patrol is proving increasingly essential—to the American economy, to American society, and to America itself.

STANDING GUARD

The mobile, uniformed branch of the INS, the Border Patrol is in the forefront in the fight to maintain the integrity of America's frontiers. This is a task of some considerable scale and complexity. The land frontiers measure 7,500 miles (12,077 km) in length, north to south, and the agency is additionally responsible for patrolling the seas around Florida and Puerto Rico. The main focus, however, is on America's land borders, and economic and political realities mean that it is the 2,000-mile (3,221-km) Mexican border that has tended to be seen as more of a problem.

Over the years, countless migrants have tried to head north from Latin America, fleeing lives of poverty and sometimes political persecution. Comparatively few, however, have felt a need to break the law to leave behind the affluence of Canada. Some have. Whether wanted criminals or non-Canadians using the country as a staging post on the way to the United States, these immigrants hoped to benefit from what they have assumed to be a less closely guarded northern frontier. Once, this was indeed the case—the supervision along both borders was surprisingly slack by modern standards, and a single agent on a horse took care of sections hundreds of miles long. Today, however, no country can afford to

**Officers of the U.S. Coast Guard found 185 Haitian migrants
crammed into this 31-foot (9-m) sailboat when they boarded it off
Elliot Key, Florida, in December 2001.**

neglect its frontiers—certainly not the world's greatest democracy
and unrivaled economic superpower. The Border Patrol today is a
large and well-organized force with state-of-the-art surveillance and
sensory equipment and weaponry—although there is still
sometimes no substitute for the agent on his horse.

THE GREAT GAME

Every afternoon along the southern frontier, units of the U.S.
Border Patrol are gearing up for another night's action. The routine

At the very foot of the frontier fence, two Mexicans lie by a fire in the chill of the desert night, waiting for the right moment to attempt their crossing into America.

may vary in details, but the ritual never ends. Agents know that tonight, as every night, there will be attempted illegal entries. "As soon as the sun goes down," writes Terry McCarthy of *Time,* "Hundreds of men, women, and children, armed with water bottles, toothbrushes, toilet paper, and perhaps phone numbers in Phoenix or Denver or Los Angeles, come walking, running, and crawling north across the border. Each night, Border Patrol agents round up 500 and next morning return them to Mexico, only to have them start all over again the following evening."

Would-be immigrants find other means of entry: some stow away in trucks or trains; others tunnel under frontier barriers or swim rivers. In Calexico, reports McCarthy, "aliens float down a stream choked with toxic chemicals and sewage, betting the Border Patrol won't jump in to pull them out."

Most illegal immigrants, however, simply walk, hoping to overwhelm America's high-tech defenses by sheer weight of numbers. And the strategy makes sense: all the searchlights and electronic

Just one of the 1.5 million apprehended annually in this sector of the southern frontier alone, an illegal alien is arrested by an officer of the Border Patrol in the Calexico Desert, outside Tijuana.

Diana Perez, an agent of the Border Patrol in Brownsville, Texas, searches a party of aliens caught attempting to enter the United States illegally in her sector.

surveillance in the world cannot hope to hold back so sustained an assault along such a long frontier by so many people.

Many people each night will be spotted from above by Border Patrol helicopters, detected from below by underground sensors, sighted at ground level through infrared night-vision goggles, or stumbled on by sheer good fortune. There will still be some, however, who slip through the net—enough to make this great game, with all its risks, seem worthwhile; enough to ensure that this crisis on the southern frontier of the United States continues indefinitely into the future.

THE ILLEGAL'S TALE

Antonio Godinez was not so much caught as rescued by the Border Patrol, who found him with a group in grave difficulties in the Arizona desert in 2001. He told his story to Tom Zeller of *The New York Times*. A native of Tepalcatepec, central Mexico, and 22 years old, he had traveled about 1,000 miles (1,610 km) since leaving his home some two weeks previously. Taking a bus to Tijuana, he first contemplated crossing the border there, but was then persuaded by local Coyotes that he stood a better chance near Nogales, Arizona, where the Border Patrol presence was reputed to be thinner. Another bus journey took him 500 miles (805 km) eastward, and there he made arrangements with a Coyote. The Coyote agreed to take him across a quiet stretch of frontier with a vanload of other illegals. Each paid $1,000 for the short ride.

It turned out to be a very short ride. Sighting a Border Patrol vehicle in the distance, the Coyote turned his contraband passengers out and fled, leaving them in the desert to fend for themselves. Questioned by the reporter, Godinez admits to having feared for his life in his two days and nights lost in the desert. Asked if he will try again, he smiles and says no—but it's by no means clear that he really means it.

Albert Fresquez, the Border Patrol agent who has just quite literally saved his life, wonders whether any of the illegals truly understand the risks involved. "He was in a lot of trouble," he says, shaking his head sadly. "These folks don't realize sometimes how far they've got to go to get anywhere, and the desert can be tough."

DIVIDED LOYALTIES?

Like many members of the Border Patrol along the southern frontier, Gloria Chávez is herself a Mexican American, sharing ethnic and cultural roots with many of those she has to arrest and exclude in the line of work. Yet while she may sympathize with the would-be immigrants, she says that she has never for a moment doubted her duty or regretted her decision to join up with the Border Patrol. "Yes, I'm a Mexican American," she tells Claudia S. Meléndez of *El Andar* magazine, "but I'm not going to let my ancestry influence me or make me bend the rules." In her three years as an agent, she has arrested more than 3,000 people—most of whom have had a similar ethnic background to her own. She respects the impulse that drives so many Mexicans northward in the attempt to better themselves—and understands why those she is forced to turn back may see her service as some kind of betrayal. Yet she herself sees no conflict; after all, she is an American. "I take a lot of pride in doing what I do, I'm honored," she concludes.

THE BORDER PATROL

Politically charged images of the "fortified frontier," of a "Berlin Wall" between the affluent North and impoverished South, give a misleading picture of the realities of life on the Mexican border. The cliché may, to some extent, hold good in and around urban areas like Tijuana—San Diego and El Paso—Ciudad Juarez, which are traditional "hot spots" for illegal entry into the United States. Here, it is true, apparently impenetrable barriers bristle with electronic

Thwarted—for the moment, at least—in their efforts to cross into America, a group of Mexican illegals is marched back for processing by officers of the U.S. Border Patrol. These men will be formally deported from the country, but once returned to Mexico, there will be nothing to stop them renewing their attempt at entry.

sensoring, sighting, and listening equipment. However, just a few miles out of town, the scene is quite different. The Border Patrol must rely on barbed wire—and its own vigilance—to keep illegal immigrants out. There is no great mystery about the methods used by the Border Patrol, although a great deal of skill and experience is required to employ them effectively. In the end, it all comes down to the twin techniques of "line watch" and "sign cutting." The first of these involves, quite literally, the watching of the line—the effective observation of the frontier so as to prevent its violation. The second involves checking for signs of illegal entry after the event and the tracking down of aliens before they can disappear into urban areas. The skills it calls upon are those of the desert hunter.

ON THE TRAIL

A cut strand of barbed wire here, a bent or broken fencepost there: often, the visible signs of entry are only too clear. The experienced

Caution—undocumented aliens crossing, warns this sign beside a busy freeway. In frontier regions, illegal immigration is a part of everyday life.

signcutter, however, can also "read" the rocky ground like a book. A glance or two is enough to confirm the passage of people—and, frequently, their number and their rate of progress. There are five main types of trace.

The first is the flattening effect of a footstep or vehicle squashing down rocks, dirt, or twigs into the desert earth. The second is any sign of regularity, which is never found in nature: the circles and other geometrical shapes left by the typical trainer-sole or tire practically scream out to the experienced tracker. The third thing to look for is any disturbance: the dislodging of stones or twigs from their proper place is clear evidence that somebody has recently passed this way. Next comes color-change: disturbed rock, soil, or vegetation tends to catch the light differently, and often this is all that sharp-eyed signcutters need to see to know they are on the trail. The fifth characteristic is transfer: anything moved out of place by a passing shoe, such as when rich mud from a ditch or arroyo turns up in an area of arid sand, for instance.

A footprint may show up in some lights, but be entirely invisible in others. The tracker learns to examine the ground carefully from a number of different angles. Some times of day are better than others. In the early morning, for instance, the disturbance of dew on grass and low shrubs may be a giveaway sign. Since certain surfaces take better tracks than others, what has been a reasonably clear trail may abruptly disappear. Those tracks that can be identified are carefully flagged with little bits of toilet paper tied to twigs, and these may help direction to be maintained until footprints can once again be seen.

Agent David Trevino of the Texas Border Patrol scours the desert landscape with high-powered binoculars, alert for any sign that illegal immigrants may have passed this way.

The identification of such immediate physical traces is the central skill of sign cutting, but trackers with talent and experience can "read" a good many more. Some may be as obvious as a discarded water bottle or candy bar wrapper, but others are harder to pin down. Ideally, signcutters learn to think themselves into the mind of the illegal immigrant. Men and women walking across country tend to take the "path of least resistance"—in rough terrain, it is often possible to guess their likely route with a fair degree of confidence. In a largely featureless landscape, unguided wayfarers have a tendency to take aim on some distant landmark. Again, the intuitive tracker may be able accurately to predict their course.

OTHER ROUTES

Some illegal immigrants from Mexico prefer the risks of being caught by officials (or even killed in accidents) to the travails of a long and arduous journey across the desert. Some hide themselves on the spur of the moment in the backs of trucks or in railroad boxcars; others are concealed with greater or lesser degrees of professionalism by organized Coyotes. Many such stowaways are

The work of the U.S. Border Patrol is not universally popular. Some civil rights groups believe they persecute essentially innocent men and women, who have been driven to break the law only by desperate poverty.

unceremoniously hauled out at border crossings, but a certain number undoubtedly make it through successfully.

The Border Patrol operates traffic checkpoints well north of the border to increase the chances of apprehending immigrants like these—as well as those who, having walked across the frontier, take to the highway to continue their journey. Suspicious-looking cars and trucks are stopped and searched and drivers' and passengers' papers thoroughly checked; buses, too, are checked for those attempting to travel without documentation. Trains are regularly stopped and searched. Illegal immigrants may be hiding as they travel, or may simply be taking their chances among the legitimate passengers.

A HIGH-TECH RESPONSE

The Border Patrol has transportation of its own. In recent years, it has been able to conduct systematic air-surveillance in certain areas, using helicopters and light aircraft. At night, helicopters with powerful searchlights often work in cooperation with ground patrols, for whom they can effectively detect and "pin down" parties of illegal immigrants in open country.

The standard means of overland transport these days is, of course, the 4 x 4 all-terrain vehicle, although some agents feel that bikes and horses have the virtue of keeping them closer to the ground. Marine patrols in coastal areas have to have fast power-launches if they are to stand a chance of keeping pace with well-equipped people smugglers. In these areas, the U.S. Coast Guard also plays an important part in sighting and detaining illegal immigrants.

FRONTLINE: ANDALUCÍA

Five would-be immigrants a day are believed to drown in the Straits of Gibraltar in the attempt to make the crossing from impoverished Africa to affluent Europe. Although only a few miles wide, the straits are rendered treacherous by swift currents and by the busy traffic of one of the world's most important shipping lanes.

Organized gangs of people smugglers charge migrants between $600 and $1,000 a time for a place in a small boat so full of passengers that it may well ride less than 12 inches (30 cm) above the waterline. Many inevitably founder or overturn, but there is still no shortage of prospective passengers: the economics of emigration are just too appealing.

Most come from Morocco, although there is a steady stream, too, from sub-Saharan Africa. They and their families will have saved for years to earn this precarious passage. Those who make it as far as Spain will find themselves at the very bottom of the social heap, toiling long hours in agriculture at half the wages of native-born Spanish farm workers. A dismal prospect? Not from their perspective. That rate of pay works out to be 10 times what they could hope to earn at home in North Africa. Many of the migrants save money to send home to their family.

In what has long been one of Spain's poorest areas, there have been several serious outbreaks of racial violence among the local population, but, despite the difficulties, the rewards for the immigrants are just too great to be resisted and the problem is likely to continue for many years.

77

THE "SMART BORDER"

"America's borders," said a White House statement issued in January 2002, "are the boundaries between the United States and the rest of the world." That may seem like a statement of the obvious, and yet it is by no means immediately clear how the nation is to address the paradox that the President's press office went on to pinpoint so precisely. On the one hand, as it said, "The massive flow of people and goods across our borders helps drive our economy." On the other, "It can also serve as a conduit for terrorists, weapons of mass destruction, illegal migrants, contraband, and other unlawful commodities."

The challenge over the next few years will be to create what analysts are calling a "Smart Border": a barrier to America's enemies, but a bridge to trade. The INS and Border Patrol will undoubtedly have their part to play, but new attitudes and new ways of thinking also will be required. In fact, there are already signs that these agencies have been responding to changing times, with fresh ideas and imaginative initiatives already much in evidence. Recent initiatives along the U.S. border have shown both the resolve of its guardians and the flexibility of their thinking. Both are going to be needed as we go forward to face the future.

Left: Border Patrol workers erect a fence along the U.S.–Mexico border. The fence will be 10 feet (3 m) tall and have a base of steel mats extending 3 feet (90 cm) underground.

RESULTS IN THE ROUND

Increasingly in recent years, the Border Patrol has measured its effectiveness not only in terms of illegal immigrants apprehended, but also in terms of pro-active programs against people-smuggling gangs. In addition, they have worked—often in cooperation with police and customs officials—to cut off supplies of illegal narcotics into the country. Since experience has shown that illegal immigrants

Vehicles line up at the Niagara Falls Border Crossing. Controls on the Canadian border are traditionally more relaxed than those to the south, but the increasing ingenuity and determination of the illegal immigrants, compounded by the threat of international terrorism since the events of September 2001, have meant a tightening of security.

The authority of the federal agent has to be backed up by the force of arms. No one can be in any doubt of the life-or-death determination of many illegal aliens.

and drugs are often smuggled in by the same people, it clearly makes sense for interested agencies to work in close collaboration. In 1999 alone, the Border Patrol seized over 29,000 pounds (13,154 kg) of cocaine and almost 1.2 million pounds (544,316 kg) of marijuana. The total street value of the drugs seized was over $1.9 billion.

OPERATION GATEKEEPER
One important initiative in this area has been Operation Gate-keeper, a deliberately high-profile program launched in southern

America's enmity with Castro's Cuba is no secret, but its opposition to any form of terrorism runs deeper. Having hijacked a boat for his escape to America, this man is promptly deported.

California. Aimed at deterring both drug- and alien-smuggling in the area, it poured resources into the policing of the border. The cornerstone of the initiative was the upping of staffing levels: the total number of agents was increased by 140 percent. The number of those specifically tasked with the inspection of border infrastructure rose by 150 percent, and their efforts were backed up by massive increases in the provision of extra fencing, underground sensors, and high-intensity lighting.

The list of improvements is almost endless. The numbers of everything, from infrared scopes to helicopters, rose dramatically. The only key statistic that actually fell was that of arrests and seizures, which plummeted to a 17-year low. This may seem curious, but from the outset, Operation Gatekeeper was intended primarily as a program of deterrence. In a sign of the sort of new-look thinking that lay behind it, the program's success was to be measured not by an increase, but by a decrease in apprehensions.

Held pending deportation proceedings at an INS facility in southern Texas, these illegal aliens will soon be on their way back to their countries of origin.

A DOOR STILL AJAR?

North Dakota-born Brent Zimmerman worked on the Mexican border for several years before coming home to help protect the frontier with Canada. This one is quiet by comparison, he admits in conversation with Dan Gunderson of *MPR News,* although that is not necessarily an advantage. With only a few hundred agents patrolling a border thousands of miles long, he and his colleagues routinely put in 21-hour days. In the Minnesota/North Dakota section patrolled from Grand Forks, 22 agents are responsible for a stretch of over 900 miles (1,450 km); his office at Pembina, North Dakota, is responsible for 100 miles (160 km)—mostly thick forest. There's no way, he admits, that they can hope to maintain the sort of surveillance levels customary on the much shorter Mexican border—but for a long time this did not seem necessary.

Now, however, says Brent, there are signs that things are getting livelier by the year as Mexicans fly to Canada, then try to get into the United States from there. One disturbing development has been the suspicion that terrorists may slip through: so long a frontier may seem almost like an open invitation. A couple of years back, says Assistant Chief Patrol Agent Lonnie Schweitzer in Grand Forks, agents arrested two Sikh terrorists in Minneapolis, "the number-one and -two wanted people in India." In the aftermath of September 11, 2001, the signs are that steps are being taken to tighten up this most exposed of America's frontiers with beefed-up staffing and surveillance equipment—but there is a lot of border there and much work still to do.

COMBINED RESOURCES

Meanwhile, throughout the United States, the INS has been working hard not only to enhance its own computer systems, but also to improve information sharing with other government agencies. For far too long, America's different law enforcement and intelligence-gathering offices have tended to go their separate ways, leaving endless gaps in the overall system in which wrongdoers

Sometimes, accidental immigrants reach our shores; here a Chinese-American officer of the USS *Boxer* translates for the captain and crew of a Taiwanese fishing boat rescued after getting into difficulties on the high seas.

ELÍAN GONZALEZ

Six-year-old Elían Gonzalez became perhaps America's most famous refugee when he was rescued by the U.S. Coast Guard off the coast of Florida in November 1999. His mother and 10 other refugees drowned when the boat taking them from Cuba sank in heavy seas. Elían's story became a major headache for the INS when a bitter dispute began in which politics and emotions came together in a highly combustible mixture.

Elían's relatives in Miami's Cuban community, pointing to the clear intentions of Elían's late mother, claimed that the boy's future simply had to lie in America. Back in Havana, however, Elían's father disagreed and angrily demanded his son's return—Cuban leader Fidel Castro orchestrated massive demonstrations in his support. Feelings ran high as father Juan Miguel Gonzalez accused America of trying to bribe his son with trips to Disney World, while Cuban-Americans accused the INS of cravenly surrendering to Communism.

The dawn raid in which the INS forcibly took Elían into protective custody was an unmitigated public-relations disaster. Photographs of the terrified boy apparently being held at gunpoint by a Border Patrol officer shocked people in both the United States and throughout the world. In fact, appearances were deceptive. Despite all the disruption, young Elían's story seems genuinely to have had what he himself regarded as a satisfactory and happy ending. So it was a job well done, even if not exactly a public-relations triumph for the INS.

Snatched from a heaving sea to find himself at the center of a political storm, Elían Gonzalez has every reason to look bewildered. The story of the six-year-old's rescue, and the diplomatic wrangling that ensued, captured the imagination of the world.

Armed INS agents storm the house in which his relations hold Elían Gonzalez. To Miami's outraged Cuban community, the conduct of this dramatic, pre-dawn raid effectively implied that the young boy's family were nothing more than criminal kidnappers.

could hide. The aim today is a "seamless" system. Increasingly, such a setup seems attainable, thanks to the awesome capacity of today's information technology. The INS's proposed entry-exit system will make it possible to track the arrivals and departures of non-U.S. citizens with far greater ease and assurance than ever before, excluding the undesirable, but speeding the admission of legitimate travelers. In this way the United States should be able to have the best of both worlds, a border open to trade and tourism but closed to terrorists and illegal immigrants.

The "militarization of the border," it has been called by an indignant Mexican government, but as far as America is concerned, good fences make good neighbors. This stretch of the border, in New Mexico, has not only been the scene for large-scale illegal entry in recent years, but has also offered an easy escape route for bandits holding up freight trains on the U.S. side.

WORKING TOGETHER

The INS has long cooperated with other agencies—the U.S. Coast Guard, for example, with whom it works to police the problem of seaborne immigration from Cuba, Haiti, and other Caribbean countries. As with overland illegal immigration rings, those responsible for the traffic in people are often involved in the smuggling of drugs and other contraband. Hence, the importance of collaboration with customs and with those federal and local law enforcement agencies responsible for fighting crime in the cities of Florida and the Gulf Coast.

This type of joint venture is going to have to become more and more the norm for all such agencies as America arms itself against the threats of the 21st century. The tragedy of September 11, 2001, and the terrifying destruction the attackers caused, has brought

Caught in the glare of the flashlight in the Calexico Desert, north of Tijuana, two more illegal aliens are apprehended by the agents of the Border Patrol.

STILL AN OPEN BORDER

There is no razor wire and no watchtowers on Fred Hollenbeck's stretch of the U.S.–Mexican border, on the banks of the Rio Grande, deep in the Big Bend National Park. The nearest official entry point is at Presidio, over 100 miles (160 km) away. However, there are 92 unofficial crossings, the vast majority of which are completely unmanned. In the absence of more serious defenses, the border is largely policed on the basis of trust—a trust that Agent Hollenbeck generally finds is not misplaced.

Citizens on both sides of the border keep an eye out on his behalf, alerting him to the presence of anyone who seems out of place or who seems in any way suspicious. Across the water, in the tiny Mexican town of Boquillas del Carmen, local people take a positive view of the work of the Border Patrol. "The U.S. is our brother," ferryman Victor Valdez told Diane Jennings of the *Dallas Morning News*. Besides, he added wryly, "Without tourists, nobody will have money to spend."

about a dramatic transformation in American attitudes. Kindled by the outrage, the country has begun gearing up for its own defense against dangers of a sort never previously envisaged.

In retrospect, however, the September 11, 2001, attacks can be seen merely to have accelerated an inevitable shift in thinking, as America redraws its boundaries, reconceiving its former limits to imagine a new frontier that is flexible, yet secure—the "Smart Border" of the future.

GLOSSARY

Anti-Semitism: an irrational dislike of Jewish people that can lead to hatred and violence against them

Asylum: the right to safe sanctuary, which a refugee is entitled to claim in another country

BORSTAR: "Border Patrol Search, Trauma, and Rescue Team"—a team of EMTs (Emergency Medical Technicians) responsible for administering emergency medical assistance to illegal immigrants who get into difficulty in the course of their border crossing

Coyote: local guide who hires out his services to Mexicans in border regions hoping to cross illegally into the United States

Democracy: a government elected to rule by the majority of a country's people

Emigration: to leave one country to move to another country

Ghetto: a part of a city where a poor or persecuted minority is forced to live

Immigration: the movement of a person or people ("immigrants") into a country; as opposed to emigration, their movement out

Internment: to hold someone, especially an immigrant, while his or her application for residence is being processed

Naturalization: the process by which a foreigner is officially "naturalized," or accepted as a U.S. citizen

Persecution: to harass or attack someone because of his or her different racial, ethnic, or religious background

Pilgrimage: to make a journey to a sacred place

Prejudice: to hold negative opinions and make unfounded judgements about a person or group of people

Racism: to dislike someone because of his or her race

Recession: a time when the economy of a country or group of countries is slow, leading to job loses and poverty

Refugee: a person forced to take refuge in a country not his or her own, displaced by war or political instability at home

Scapegoat: a person or group of people who are unfairly blamed for something

Segregationist: someone who wants ethnic, religious, and racial groups to live and work separately, usually to the advantage of the stronger group

UNHCR: the United Nations High Commissioner for Refugees is the internationally recognized office in charge of promoting the protection of refugees; it is a part of the United Nations organization—a New York-based body set up after World War II to foster cooperation and peace between the nations of the world

CHRONOLOGY

1865: Individual states start passing their own piecemeal legislation imposing laws and limits on immigration; prior to this, no serious attempt had been made to control the flow.

1875: Supreme Court decides that the regulation of immigration is the responsibility of federal, rather than state, government.

1882: Chinese Exclusion Act bars entry to Chinese immigrants for a 10-year period.

1891: Immigration Act bars polygamists and "persons convicted of crimes of moral turpitude" from admission to the United States, along with individuals suffering from dangerously contagious diseases. Immigration Service set up to police the new rules.

1892: January 2, Federal Immigration Station at Ellis Island, New York Harbor, opens.

1906: Basic Naturalization Act standardizes the naturalization process U.S.-wide, bringing it out of state and into federal control; Naturalization Service is set up to administer procedures.

1917: Immigration Act sets minimum literacy standards for all immigrants, demanding that they be able to read and write in their own language; in practice, this favors middle-class European immigrants with good levels of education.

1921: Immigration Act, known as the "Quota Act," stipulates that new immigrants can be admitted only in numbers proportional to their representation in earlier census findings; this clearly favors those belonging to long-established—and mainly European—ethnic communities.

1924: Immigration Act, known as the Johnson-Reed Act, reinforces the provisions of the Act of 1921; illegal immigration rises throughout this period, as possibilities for legal entry are progressively foreclosed.

1933: Immigration Service and Naturalization Service merge into a single Immigration and Naturalization Service (INS).

1941–1945: America is involved in Second World War; INS is in charge of detaining "aliens" (especially Japanese-Americans) in internment camps and guarding borders against enemy spies.

1950: Statute of the United Nations High Commissioner for Refugees passed by resolution of UN General Assembly; it stipulates that those with a "well-founded fear of persecution" have a legal right to claim protection.

1986: Immigration Reform and Control Act lets INS act against employers found to have hired undocumented aliens; since the law also gives certain illegal aliens the opportunity of regularizing their position, it is seen as representing a decisive shift toward a more compassionate immigration policy.

FURTHER INFORMATION

USEFUL WEB SITES

www.ins.usdoj.gov.: The INS's own web site, this is an immensely valuable resource. It gives information on every aspect of U.S. immigration, both past and present, and includes the most up-to-the-minute, practical guidance for new immigrants. There is also an online museum of immigration history for school students, as well as details of the work of the agency's key departments in different parts of the country—including the recent operations of the Border Patrol.

FURTHER READING

Various books celebrate America's modern diversity and multicultural history.

Daniels, Roger. *Coming to America: A History of Immigration and Ethnicity in American Life.* New York: Harper Collins, 1990.

Nevins, Joseph and Mike Davis. *Operation Gatekeeper: The Rise of the "Illegal Alien" and the Remaking of the U.S.-Mexico Boundary.* New York: Routledge, 2001.

Pipher, Mary Bray. *The Middle of Everywhere: The World's Refugees Come to Our Town.* New York: Harcourt Brace, 2002.

Takaki, Ronald T. *A Different Mirror: A History of Multicultural America.* Boston: Little, Brown, 1993.

Takaki, Ronald T. *A Larger Memory: A History of Our Diversity, With Voices.* Boston: Little, Brown, 1998.

Takaki, Ronald T. *A Larger Memory: A History of Our Diversity, With Voices*. Boston: Little, Brown, 1998. This is an anthology of personal testimony from throughout American history and across the entire American ethnic spectrum.

ABOUT THE AUTHOR

Michael Kerrigan was born in Liverpool, England, and educated at St Edward's College, from where he won an Open Scholarship to University College, Oxford. He lived for a time in the United States, spending time first at Princeton, followed by a period working in publishing in New York. Since then, he has been a freelance writer and journalist, with commissions across a wide range of subjects, but with a special interest in social policy and defense issues. Within this field, he has written on every region of the world. His work has been published by a number of leading international educational publishers including the BBC, Dorling Kinderslcy, Time-Life, and Reader's Digest Books. His work as a journalist includes regular contributions to the *Times Literary Supplement*, London, as well as a weekly column in the *Scotsman* newspaper, Edinburgh, where he now lives with his wife and their two small children.

INDEX

References in italics refer to illustrations